What We Carry

By
Mica Boyd Johnston

Table of Contents

Dedication

Dedicated to my five children - Sunny, Russell, Danny, Nicole & Steven, the heartbeats of my life.

No matter where you go or who you become, my love for you will remain constant and unshaken, as eternal as the seasons themselves. Through every trial and every joy, I will always be here, loving you in every form, forever more.

Acknowledgment

To my children and grandchildren—

You are my light, my reason, and my greatest joy. Every word in this book carries a part of you. Thank you for giving me the honor of being your mother and grandmother. I hope you always feel how deeply you are loved.

To the friends who listened, encouraged, and believed in me even when I doubted myself—your kindness and support helped bring this book to life. Thank you for your open hearts and steady presence.

To the readers—thank you for picking up this book and giving my words a place to land. I hope they bring comfort, clarity, and connection to your own journey.

And to the quiet moments, the long walks, the early mornings, and the memories that stayed with me—thank you for the inspiration. You helped shape every page.

With all my heart.

About the Author

Mica Boyd Johnston is a writer and traveler whose poetry and memoirs are steeped in memory, movement, and meaning. Her words reflect a lifelong journey—one filled with quiet strength, open roads, and deep emotional truth.

She is the author of Brownie, a memoir that chronicles her early years of constant travel across the United States, and My Magical Trip to Ireland, a heartfelt reflection on fulfilling a lifelong dream. Her newest book, The Road to Duchesne, currently in editing, continues the story of her childhood on the move. From there, she plans to write about the next leg of her journey—Cheyenne, Wyoming.

Mica intends to travel until she can no longer travel and write until she can no longer write. She finds joy in spring mornings, in blooming wildflowers, and in the simple beauty that reminds us that there is always more to see, more to feel, and more to say.

Introduction

These are poems from my very soul.

Each one holds a piece of who I am—what I've seen, what I've felt, what I've carried across the years. This collection reflects the moments that shaped me, the lessons I've lived, and the love I continue to give.

What We Carry is divided into four chapters: *What We're Given, What We Endure, What We Let Go,* and *What We Keep.* Within those pages are stories—some whispered, some loud—that speak to family, aging, identity, hope, sorrow, and joy. These poems are my way of making sense of the weight we all hold and the light we continue to seek.

I wrote this with my children and grandchildren in my heart and for anyone who's ever wondered if their voice still matters. It does. Yours does.

Thank you for holding these words. Thank you for walking this road with me.

— Mica Boyd Johnston

Page Blank Intentionally

Chapter 1: What We're Given

Grandchildren

Life's path may twist.
And skies turn gray.
But have no fear,
I'll be near,
With compass and tissue
to wipe away tears.

Headed to Ireland 2024

In every Irish melody Lies an echo of the free.
In America's tapestry, a thread of green you'll see.
May the journey that I now embark,
be filled with discovery and lighted, spark.
Ireland, oh Ireland, my ancestor's home,
to the land of the green, this is where I will soon roam.

MICA BOYD JOHNSTON

This is what I know

I was given many things in life—
a roof to call my own,
water that runs clean and quiet,
a job that paid the bills
and kept the lights humming.

But the greatest gift?
Five beating hearts—
three boys,
two girls,
each one a world unto themselves.

I didn't always get it right.
There were times I stumbled,
times I raised my voice
when I should've listened.
I didn't know what I didn't know.

But I made sure
you had a place to sleep,
food to fill your belly,
and a mother who tried—
even when she was tired,
even when she was learning.

And now,
as you've grown into your own lives,
I try to show you
in the ways I know how—
that you are my everything.
That no one could ever
take your place.

You were the gift
I didn't know I'd need—
the reason I kept going,

the reason I still do.

And if love
can be passed down
like an heirloom,
know this:
what I was given,
I give to you—
with more heart
than I ever had to start.

What We Are Given

My father gave me silence—
not the kind that breaks,
but the kind that holds.
He taught me how to carry
what I could never say.

He worked with hands that never slowed,
a voice that didn't ask but told.
From him, I learned that strength
was something earned,
not shown.

My mother gave me quiet courage—
though I didn't see it then.
I mistook her softness for surrender,
but now I know
it takes strength to stay
when the world pulls you away.

She faded with each move,
drifting farther from her roots,
until her laughter lived
only in old phone calls
and memories of kin.

My parents gave me work
before they gave me rest.
They gave me grit,
they gave me fire.
They gave me the tools
to hold myself up—
no matter how heavy I became.

Where Our Story Begins

In dusty records, secrets long concealed,
ancestry's tale is slowly revealed.
With every step through history we tread,
seeking the roots from which we spread.

Names and faces from the past,
whisper stories meant to last.
Faded ink and photographs,
echoes of our lineage's path.

From distant lands across the swell,
our ancestors' journeys rise and tell—
of struggles faced and battles won,
of dreams begun beneath the sun.

Their triumphs, fears, and hopes reside.
Within our hearts, deep and wide.
A legacy of courage runs within,
a thread of strength, from kin to kin.

In genealogy's sacred quest,
we find the ties that bind us best.
Connecting dots to where we start,
we map the bloodline of our heart.

For in our roots, we learn our place—
ancestry's light, our guiding grace.
Its tapestry we proudly bear,
a story woven deep with care.

The Cliffs of Moher

Upon the edge of Ireland's west,
where waves and wind never come to rest.
Stand the Cliffs of Moher,
so grand and alluring,
a natural wonder, ancient and enduring.
They rise from the sea.
A sheer wall of might.
Combined with the Green of Ireland's delight.
A history rich with tales untold,
of battles so fierce and warriors so bold.
The Puffins dance on the breeze with ease,
nature's chorus, wild and free.
A stunning beauty, raw and pure,
mist kissed rocks, Ireland's allure.
Where emerald cliffs meet the pale blue sky,
you'll find a peace no money can buy.

Learning to Be Grateful

Our brains were built for survival—
to scan for danger,
to notice what's missing
before what's given.
It kept our ancestors alive,
but it keeps *us*
restless.

We are taught to want more,
to earn more,
to prove we deserve to be here.
Gratitude can feel like stopping,
and stopping
feels like losing.

We run toward a finish line
we never chose,
measuring our worth
in titles, square footage,
bank balances,
busy calendars.

We fear that contentment
will make us soft.
That resting means surrender.
We say we're fine,
but we don't believe it
until there's nothing left to chase.

Many of us learned this
from parents who survived lack—
from grandparents who bore struggle
like a second skin.
They didn't always say
"you should want more,"

but they lived it,
and we listened
with our eyes.

So, we confused peace with laziness.
We mistook gratitude for weakness.
We thought rest meant giving up—
but it never did.

Gratitude is the moment
you finally see the life
you built with your bare hands
and say,
"This is enough.
I am enough."

Not because I stopped trying,
but because I stopped running
from the truth
that everything I needed
was already here.

Childhood's Realm

In childhood's realm, where dreams take flight,
A world of wonder, pure and bright.
Imagination knows no bounds—
in innocence, a treasure is found.

With laughter's grace and curious eyes,
beneath the vast, clear blue skies,
they danced through days so wild and free—
childhood's sweet, enchanted glee.

Though years may pass and time may fade,
the memories of that joy cascade.
Childhood's magic, forever stored—
in our hearts, a treasure adored.

"I thought I was being uprooted—but I was being expanded."

— *Mica Boyd Johnston*

The Gift of the Road

When I was young,
we were always going—
packing, driving, leaving,
starting over again.
The road was home
more than any house ever was.

I didn't understand it then—
the constant shifting.
The ache of goodbye,
the nerves before hello.
But looking back,
it wasn't just movement.
It was a gift.

I saw this country
not on maps,
but through wide windows
and weary eyes.

Desert sunsets painted in purple and fire.
Snow-capped peaks like dreams
against a blue so deep it hushed you.
Forests that whispered secrets
you could almost hear.
Oceans that stretched like promises.
Rivers so wide,
it seemed no one could ever cross.

And the food—
homemade tortillas on the reservation,
thick juicy steak in Cheyenne,
tacos fresh each morning,
trout pulled from the stream
and grilled before the sun went down.

I saw rainbows—
so many I stopped counting.
License plates like puzzle pieces
from all fifty states.
And people—
tall and blond,
short and dark,
laughing, crying,
talking in rhythms I'd never heard before.

The Germans in the Northwest,
the cowboys of the plains,
the Spanish voices echoing in the desert,
the Valley Girls of L.A.,
the slow drawl of Boston,
the crisp click of Connecticut words.

As a child,
I thought the moving was the loss.
Now I know—
it was the gaining.
The gathering.

Growing up on the road
gave me more than a view—
it gave me insight.
Into people.
Into places.
Into the soul of the U.S. of A.

And for that,
I am forever grateful.

Chapter 2: What We Endure

MICA BOYD JOHNSTON

Different Roads

I pictured who you might become—
each of you,
rooted in strength,
steady with purpose,
a spark behind your eyes
that couldn't be dimmed.

Not because I needed perfection—
but because I gave you all I had.
I wanted you to rise,
to stand firm,
to know who you were
and never let the world shake it loose.

I pointed to the light.
Every day, every mile,
I did my best
to lead you toward something true.

But you walked your own road.

Some of you press forward,
making something steady of your days—
work, family, love that holds.
And I am proud.
So proud.

And some of you…
you drift.
Not lost,
but far from the strength I hoped you'd carry.
Far from the vision
I once held close.

I ask myself questions
that don't have answers—

WHAT WE CARRY

how can such different paths unfold
from the same heart that held you all?

But I won't give up.
Not on you.
Not ever.

Because a mother's love
isn't built on what you become—
it's built on the fact
that you are mine.

And I'll always be here—
standing at the crossroads,
light in my hands,
in case one day
you need help
finding your way back.

Friends No More

Within the walls, where dreams took flight.
Ambitions hunger devoured the light.
For friendships, flame cannot thrive on deceit,
I'm leaving behind the pain, I'll retreat.
You, my friend, transformed unkind,
fires of betrayal burned entwined.
A puppeteer pulling strings unseen,
all loyalty shattered like glass so keen.
I release the weight of our shared past,
I'll walk away, my heart unmasked.
At this chapter's end, a new dawn awaits,
for true friends, don't manipulate or berate.
Farewell old friend, the ties now severed.
I'll rise above, my spirit untethered.

Is Life a Struggle?

Building the life I have been dreaming of,
climbing the endless stairs of obstacles.
Tired of all these responsibilities.
Who made life this hard and impossible?
Who set the path so steep and winding?
Dear God, where is the silver lining?
Is it in the journey that we find our strength,
it's challenges, it's breadth, it's length.
Perhaps the trials shape our soul,
each burden carved to make us whole.
Through weary steps and nights so long,
we find our fire, we grow more strong.
Not just in victory but in the fight,
not in the ease, but in the night.
For even storms will pass away,
and dawn will bring a brighter day.

Odessa, Texas

In the hundred-degree furnace, Odessa stands,
a dusty oil town where dreams meet demands.
The money flows like crude, hard-earned, and raw,
etching young faces with lines deeply flawed.
License plates from every state line, the many streets,
a symphony of wanderlust where many cultures meet.
In this desert melting pot, ambition fuels the fire,
fortunes rise and fall and many dreams dare to aspire.
The pursuit of prosperity drives their arrival,
dreams and sweat forge a path to survival.
From every corner of the earth, they converge,
in this desert canvas, their stories all emerge.
Forty-eight years now, under the scorching sun, we also arrived in
Odessa seeking a new dawn.
My father and mother made of grit and sweated brow,
chased opportunities picture as their dreams would allow.
Though my parents have departed, their legacy remains.
Woven into the fabric of the sunbaked Odessa plains.
Like the many before them, all looking for work,
there will be many people after, each with their own quirk.
That's the great thing about our own melting pot,
you never know what kind of characters you've got.
In the tapestry of Odessa, woven with thread so diverse,
each person adds color to our unique place on earth.

The Mirror

Who is this woman I see today,
in the mirror's quiet, silver-gray?
Green eyes, once bright, now faded light,
a face that's weathered silent fight.
Streaks of gray where red once burned,
soft lines earned from lessons learned.
I don't recall this face I see—
she isn't how I used to be.
The girl I knew was fierce, alive,
with dreams so big, she'd leap and dive.
Hair like fire, wild and long,
a laugh, a spark, a morning song.
But somewhere, time slipped out of view,
too slow to notice, too fast to undo.
And now my bones creak with the years,
my mornings start with aches and fears.
Maybe it's food. Maybe the wine.
Maybe I crossed some unseen line.
Whatever it is, I feel the weight—
the drag of days that start too late.
I love my kids, my grandkids too,
I give my all—like I'm meant to do.
But after work, I just want rest,
a quiet chair, a softer chest.
I used to care for flowers and flair,
candles lit and perfect air.
Now, I sit and wonder why
the will to rise has passed me by.
But this is not the final page—
not the end of love or stage.
There's more to find; I feel it near—
a flicker, not yet clear.
Maybe not gardens, maybe not gold,

but something new, both bright and bold.
A spark that waits for me to see—
a different dream, a gentler me.
And though this mirror shows the years,
the lines, the loss, the quiet tears—
it doesn't show what's still inside,
the fire I've never set aside.
It doesn't show my steady flame,
the rising strength I cannot name,
the hope that hums beneath my skin,
the will to fall and rise again.
So, I will search, and I will find
what stirs the soul, what frees the mind.
I'm still becoming—watch me burn.
The fire is mine, and it returns.

A Woman's Battle

I sit in the meeting,
my ideas lined up like soldiers—
disciplined, sharp,
ready for battle.
You ignore them.
Then, repeat them.
And the room applauds
because it came from your mouth.
I don't flinch.
I don't fold.
I let you speak over me
and mark the silence like a scar.
I've climbed here
on no one's back.
Worked full days
and longer nights.
Built everything I have
while raising lives and making dinner.
You think a man opened the door for me?
You think I'm here because I smiled
or because someone owed me a favor.
You don't see the cost.
You don't ask.
You wouldn't understand it if you did.
I walk in
knowing I won't be heard.
Still, I speak.
I speak because I earned the right.
And I don't apologize.
Not anymore.
I don't cry.
Not then. Not now.
I've buried softer things

so, I could survive here.
I don't want your respect.
I demand it.
And if I don't get it—
I keep going anyway.
I am not yours to break.
I never was.

"I have carried every version of myself like a suitcase packed with dreams."

— Mica Boyd Johnston

MICA BOYD JOHNSTON

The Dreams That Change

When I was five,
I wanted a little radio—
one I could carry,
with shiny dials
and songs that played just for me.
When I was ten,
I wanted a puppy—
a small, warm thing
to follow me home
and love me best.
At fifteen,
I just wanted to go back—
to California,
to sunshine and something
that felt like home.
At twenty-seven,
I wanted a big house
for all my children—
a place with space
and laughter in every room.
At forty,
I wanted a better job—
more money, more recognition,
more something
to prove I was enough.
At fifty-five,
I wasn't sure
what I wanted anymore.
At sixty,
I wanted to travel.
And this time,
I did.
My dreams are always changing—

WHAT WE CARRY

softening, shifting.
Not because I failed
but because I grew.
Because the world got bigger
and my heart did too.
I no longer crave
the radio,
or the puppy,
or the move,
or the paycheck,
or the house full of voices.
I remember them all—
each one clear in my mind.
The little girl who begged,
the teenager who dreamed,
the mother who gave,
the woman who searched.
Dreams change
because we do.
But still,
I might find that little radio someday—
and when I do,
I just might buy it.

"We are the living proof that our ancestors existed—and endured."

— Unknown

From Kin to Kin

Vast oceans and continents wide,
carry stories the winds confide.
Tales that span through time and space,
with pride in roots—a steadfast embrace.
Generations passed, across distant lands,
identity and heritage held in their hands.
Stories told from kin to kin,
each memory a cherished win.
With roots that anchor, strong and true,
their legacy—a timeless view.
From distant shores and lands afar,
the echoes of pride shine like a star.
As time drifts on, stories fade—
entire branches lost in shade.
But I hold tight to what remains,
to whispers carried in my veins.
I may never find your name,
your face, your story, your rightful claim—
but I am thankful every day
for the path you paved, the price you paid.
I won't let this branch be lost,
not to silence, not to cost.
I'll carry you in all I do—
your blood, your strength, your truth, your view.
Through generations, tales unfold—
a legacy of identity,
a story
to be told.

MICA BOYD JOHNSTON

The Ache to Belong

There is a fire in the heart
of those who were scattered—
a burning desire
to know where we come from,
to trace our stories back
to something ancient,
something whole.
We grow up hearing names
of countries we've never seen—
Ireland. Scotland. Germany.
Whispers of great-grandparents
and crossings over oceans.
We hold onto them
like heirlooms,
like sacred things.
But when we reach out—
hoping to be welcomed,
hoping to be seen—
we are met
with laughter.
Dismissal.
Mockery.
"You're not really Irish."
"You're not German."
"You're American. Just let it go."
They don't understand
how deeply we've longed
to belong somewhere.
To someone.
To feel less
adrift.
We say, "My ancestors came from there"
because we carry

WHAT WE CARRY

the silence of those who left.
We stitch together
a patchwork of memory and myth
because it's all we have.
It's heartbreaking—
to be treated like strangers
in the places we called home
in our hearts.
I thought we were family.
I thought we were the same.
But maybe this ache
is something only
the lost understand.
Maybe the rootless
search harder
because we must.
And maybe,
just maybe,
we are building a new kind of belonging—
one that doesn't ask permission
to remember.

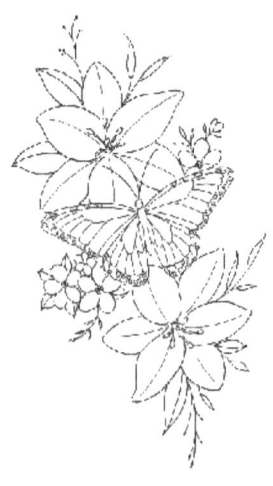

Chapter 3:
What We Let Go

"I chased efficiency like it was survival. Now I'm learning that peace has its own kind of power."

— Mica Boyd Johnston

The Pace

There was a pace
I felt I had to keep—
as if falling behind
meant falling apart.
I rose early,
moved quickly,
cleaned corners no one saw,
and learned everything
before I was asked.
Fast was safety.
Fast was survival.
Fast was the way I stayed
ahead of questions,
ahead of disappointment.
The pace with which
I felt I had to keep up
was never mine.
It was borrowed
from worry,
from worthiness,
from watching others
slip behind
and be left.
I thought slowing down
was stopping.
That rest
was a kind of failure
you had to earn.
But now—
now I know that slower
is also strong.
That presence
does not mean pause,

WHAT WE CARRY

it means
I am here
in this moment,
not racing through it.
The pace I keep
is still mine—
but now I choose
when to push,
and when to breathe.
Not to stay ahead of myself,
but to stay ready—
sharp,
strong,
present.

Jacob

You were light.
Before anything else,
that's what I remember.
The way you lit up a room—
not loud,
not demanding,
just warm.
Just… good.
You were kind
in ways the world forgets to be.
A big brother who listened,
a grandson who stayed close.
You made people feel seen.
And somehow—
We didn't see your pain.
I knew you carried a lot.
I just didn't know how much.
I believed
you would work through it.
You were so strong—
we all thought so.
But now,
we carry the silence you left behind.
I miss you
in the quiet corners of the day,
in your father's tired eyes,
in the way your siblings
look away when your name is spoken.
The world moves forward,
but something inside us doesn't.
It's been years.
But the ache doesn't know that.
It lives with us.

WHAT WE CARRY

Not every second,
but always.
And I will never understand.
Never.
I gave up trying.
That's what I let go of—
the idea that I'll ever make sense of it.
What I won't let go of
is you.
Your laugh.
Your kindness.
The light you gave
without ever asking for it back.
You were the best of us.
And we will spend
the rest of our lives
carrying your name
in everything good we do.

MICA BOYD JOHNSTON

When Did I Stop Being Me?

It didn't happen all at once.
There was no crash,
no sharp turn in the road.
Just a slow, silent drift
away from myself.

I let go of little things—
a laugh too loud,
a dream too bold,
clothes I loved but someone teased,
books that made me feel too much.

Piece by piece,
I tucked myself away
to fit into spaces
that weren't made for me.

Was it being a girl
in a world that praised quiet women?
Was it childhood,
learning early
that approval came with a price?

Or was it love—
the kind that asks you to shrink
just a little,
until one day you disappear
into someone else's vision of you?

I traded joy
for belonging.
Fire
for acceptance.
Truth
for peace in the room.

WHAT WE CARRY

And only now,
with time and stillness as my witness,
do I hear the sound
of my own voice,
returning.

I see the girl I once was—
fierce, strange,
brimming with magic
no one had the right to steal.

I miss her.
And I want her back.
Not to go back in time—
but to gather what was mine
and carry it forward,
this time
on my own terms.

MICA BOYD JOHNSTON

Like Chalk in the Rain

We moved when the engine called,
when Dad's job pulled us east or west—
no warning, no wrapping up,
just boxes packed and hearts unaddressed.

No goodbyes in the schoolyard light,
no last looks back at quiet streets.
Friends disappeared like chalk in rain,
new names forgotten just as quick.

The towns blurred into one long drive,
a restless map of starts and ends.
I learned to sit with silence deep,
to never need a lifelong friend.

I'd step into each brand-new hall,
a stranger with a practiced smile,
unsure if this would be the place
I'd call my own—for just a while.

Sometimes I whispered lies to fit,
or hung back shy, too tired to try.
Because what's the point of letting in
a world you know you'll soon deny?

And so, I let go, time and again,
of homes, of faces, and of names.
I carried on, a child unseen,
rebuilding self in shifting frames.

But in that trail of left-behind,
a quiet strength began to grow—
I learned to carry only me,
and leave the rest where I must go.

The Ones I Couldn't Carry

I carried five hearts in one worn soul,
my arms too full, my world out of control.
The weight of days, the ache of night,
no light ahead, no strength to fight.

A good man with a quiet aim,
but our dreams no longer looked the same.
He hunted peace in woods and streams,
I chased my breath and buried dreams.

A mother torn, not by desire,
but by a house half-filled with fire.
I left with three, the older ones,
and kissed goodbye my youngest son and daughter.

Three and five—they watched me go.
I prayed they'd never truly know
the storm inside, the breaking part,
the guilt that clawed beneath my heart.

They say I left. And maybe so.
But I never let their memories go.
I called. I wrote. I made the drive.
Each summer, I felt more alive.

Years passed. They came back home.
Still, some look at me like stone.
But I have stories they never see—
of nights I wept silently.

I let go once to stay alive.
But I held their names inside my life.
Now, I let go of shame and fear—
and speak the truth they need to hear.

The Ones I May Never Find

A passion for heritage, an endless universe,
in dusty archives, through time I traverse.
Ancestry's mysteries I strive to revive,
with burning fervor, into the past I dive.

Each document a clue, a thread to unwind,
I seek the stories of those left behind.
Names and places, stories suppressed,
in my heart's embrace, they find their rest.

The thrill of discovery, the thrill of the hunt,
ancestry's riddle is my soul's font.
With passion as my compass, I persist—
this lifelong search, I can't resist.

Though oceans and time may keep them afar,
I follow their trail like a guiding star.
For even in silence, I still hold tight.
To the ones I may never bring to light.

"Sometimes the hardest goodbye is the one that sets you free."

— Unknown

What I Let Go

You were once my closest friend—
the person I laughed with,
cried to,
trusted.
And then,
you broke it.
The friendship.
The bond.
Me.
I was so mad—
for years,
for too long.
I carried the weight of it,
the sting,
the loss,
the disbelief.
I replayed it,
revised it,
wished it had gone different.
But somewhere in the middle
of that grief,
the universe whispered—
let go.
And I did.
And in that space,
you used to take up,
something new grew:
Books.
Journeys.
Words.
Wonder.
I found myself
becoming someone

WHAT WE CARRY

I hadn't seen in years—
creative, open,
at peace.
I still wish
things had been different.
But it doesn't make me mad anymore.
I feel sorry for you now—
but it's no longer my weight to carry.
I have a new path—
and it feels
like freedom.

Built Into Me

I've spent a lifetime
trying to steer the people I love
in the right direction.
"Do this."
"Don't do that."
"Watch out for the curve in that road."
I thought I was helping.
Maybe I was.
But sometimes I wonder
was I trying to guide them,
or protect myself
from watching someone I love fall?
It wasn't judgment.
It was love.
It still is.
This need to guide,
to warn,
to protect—
it was built into me.
Passed down in worried glances,
in stories half-told,
in the way my people braced for the worst
while hoping for the best.
Because we care.
Because we've lived.
Because we know how hard the fall is—
and how long it takes to get up.
Because part of us thinks:
If I can just say the right thing,
maybe they won't hurt like I did.
But the truth is,
people learn when they are ready.
And that's the hardest part.

WHAT WE CARRY

I see it now—
in my kids,
in my grandkids.
That same urgency.
That same ache
to fix, to guide, to soften the blows
before they land.
Did they learn that from me?
Maybe.
Probably.
I still find myself
offering advice,
nudging gently,
trying to spare them from the pain
I carried for years.
But maybe—
just maybe—
the time has come
to sit beside them instead of standing in front.
To walk with them,
not ahead.
To trust that the same fire
that carried me
will carry them, too.

To my children and grandchildren. The only ones who matter.
"Who you choose to walk with shapes the road you take."

— Mica Boyd Johnston

Who You Walk With

People will see you
through the company you keep.

It's not always fair,
but it's always true.

You might be kind,
honest,
gentle,
smart—
but if you walk with trouble,
people will see trouble
before they see you.

So, choose your circle carefully.
If you hang with thugs
in the schoolyard,
that's who you become.
Even if you never meant to.

But if you stay close
to those who dream big,
who study hard,
who respect their parents,
who see a future—
you'll start to see yours too.

Because who you walk with
will shape how you walk.
And where you end up.

I'm not telling you
who to be.
I'm just asking you
to look around
and ask yourself:

Do these people lift me up—
or drag me down?

I've seen the difference.
I've lived the consequences.
That's why I'm telling you this.

Because I love you.
Because I believe in you.
Because I want the world
to see the best in you—
the way I do.

Chapter 4:
What We Keep

MICA BOYD JOHNSTON

Embers Never Die

The fire always burned within,
the passion was always there.
Even when life got in the way,
it didn't mean it wasn't there.
Although the flame burned low,
the embers never died,
The dreams once vivid during youth,
now fan a rising tide.
For the heart that holds the fire,
and refuses to let it die,
will find in every obstacle,
another reason to try.
A fire that burns within,
does not disappear with age.
Within the soul it burns,
as bright as the very first day.
So, let the years come and do as they may,
the fire within will burn anyway.
It's the reason for being that we all endeavor,
a flame once lit, will burn forever.

Morning

In the hush of dawn's embrace,
when the world still dreams in twilight space.
No rush, no glamour, just gentle grace,
daybreak weaves its delicate lace.
The quiet and calm cradle of dawn,
where stars retreat, and shadows yawn.
Let us linger in this quiet hour,
where hope begins like a newborn flower.

There is No Cage

When you wake up, the future is yours to create.
There is no yesterday, no past, no truth to negate.
The page is blank and waiting; grab your pencil or pen.
All doors are open.
You just have to begin.
Find the desire that's deep in your soul.
Open that door and release the flow.
Embrace the dawn and dare to dream.
Dance your own rhythm.
Shine your own beam.
You are the artist, and life is your stage.
Write with abandonment.
There is no cage.

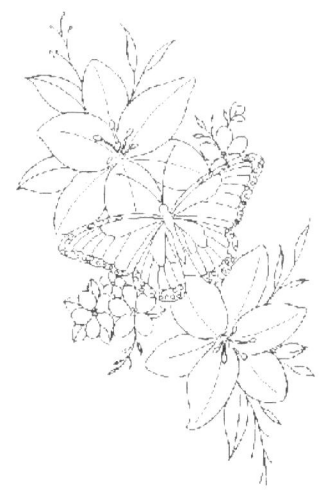

Experience One Beautiful Thing a Day

Feel the warmth of the sun on your face,
smell the aroma of freshly brewed coffee's embrace.
Take a moment to appreciate a blooming flower,
hear the sound of laughter, a joyful power.
Taste the sweetness of a ripe, juicy fruit.
Watch the gentle flow of a river, so astute.
Enjoy the calmness of a quiet evening's sway,
read a few pages of a favorite book each day.
Savor the comfort of a cozy blanket tight,
observe the vibrant colors of a sunset's light.
Listen to the rhythm of raindrops on the roof,
relish the feeling of sand between toes, the truth.
Notice the intricate patterns of butterfly wings,
delight in the crispness a fresh breeze brings.
Witness the playful antics of a pet's display,
experience the tranquility of a garden's way.
Marvel at the architecture of an old building's grace,
feel the refreshing coolness of water on your face.
Enjoy the taste of a homemade meal's array,
listen to a favorite song or music's gentle play.
Experience one beautiful thing a day,
let these moments of joy in your heart stay.

"Let it rain. I am home in the hush."

— Mica Boyd Johnston

Rain

The clouds arrive without demand,
soft-footed on the morning hush.
No thunder, no clamor—
just the tender tap of grace
on rooftops and windowsills.
In this quiet drizzle,
there's magic unfurled.
Rain showers bringing peace
to the chaotic world.
Let the rain play its symphony,
let it compose,
while we wrap ourselves
in warm thoughts and repose.
Petrichor, that golden fluid,
that runs through the veins of the gods,
showering down on our little haven,
we escape our flashy and veiled facades.
Just for a moment
our true selves revealed,
all the world is right,
all the world is healed.
The kettle hums in the kitchen,
a sweater waits draped on a chair.
Even time slows to listen
to the whisper of water in the air.
Let the world rush elsewhere—
we are tucked between seconds,
held gently in the hush
of a rain-kissed morning.

MICA BOYD JOHNSTON

The Flower Garden

In gardens, fields, and meadows fair,
a rainbow of colors, rich and rare.
Blossoms sway in the springtime breeze,
awakening from the winter freeze.
Petals soft as a baby's touch—
in their beauty, we find so much.
A vibrant burst of shades and hues,
nature's artistry, a brilliant muse.
Roses red with passion's fire,
daisies pure, like heart's desire.
Tulips reaching for the sky—
in the language of flowers, we can't deny.
Lilies elegant in their grace,
sunflowers with a sunny face.
Each bloom tells a tale untold
of nature's wonders, pure and bold.
So, let us cherish these gifts of earth—
in their presence, we find our worth.
For in a garden fraught with bowers,
we discover life's sweetest hours.

"Youth gave us dreams—age gives us the keys."

— Mica Boyd Johnston

MICA BOYD JOHNSTON

The Road Still Calls

They said the best came early—
that wild youth was where the fire lived.
But they never told us
how bright the flame can burn
once we stop dimming it for others.
Now,
we have maps scattered across countertops,
marked in ink and daydreams.
New cities whisper our names
in accents, we've yet to hear.
The bags are lighter,
but the hearts are heavier
with wisdom, wonder,
and just the right amount of daring.
This isn't slowing down—
it's gearing up
with the good shoes,
the passport,
the freedom to say yes
without asking anyone's permission.
We've traded curfews for sunrise flights,
late-night calls for ocean air.
And best of all—
we know how to linger,
how to taste,
how to talk to strangers
and turn them into stories.
So no—
life hasn't passed us by.
It's waving us forward
with open roads
and endless skies.
This is the magic we keep—

WHAT WE CARRY

the thrill of what's still possible.
And this time,
we get to choose
everything.

How Will They Remember Me?

How will they remember me,
when the years stretch long
and I'm no longer a phone call away?

Will they know
that I loved them
with everything I had—
not in grand gestures,
but in the quiet ways
I carried what they couldn't?

Will they remember
that I worked for all of it—
every comfort,
every corner of peace,
earned with hands that never stopped moving
and a mind that never stopped learning?

I hope they see
that I was someone they could follow,
someone whose footsteps were firm
because they were made with purpose.

I was the smart one.
The one they came to
when something needed fixing,
when something needed understanding.
The one who made room for their burdens,
even when they never saw the weight I held.

I hope they remember me
as the helper—
always willing,
always there,
not just in presence
but in heart.

Full Circle

I look back now
and see how far I've come—
through storms I didn't think I'd weather,
through nights that felt too heavy
to ever lead to morning.
And yet,
here I am.
I didn't do it alone.
There were people—
quiet voices,
steady hands,
gentle reminders
that I could keep going
even when I couldn't see the road.
They gave me strength
when I had none.
They gave me space
to breathe,
to think,
to gather the pieces.
They gave me
the mental clarity
to keep fighting
when the world felt too loud
to make sense.
And now,
because of them,
I rise with purpose.
Not just to live—
but to lift.
I will help those
who need a hand,
a voice,

a chance.
I will be what someone once was for me.
A light.
A bridge.
A steady place to land.
Because gratitude isn't just a feeling—
it's a calling.
And so,
to those who held me up,
to those who never let me fall,
to those who believed in me
when I barely believed in myself—
thank you.